The Phraseological Units That Shape Our Perception of Life

Iskandarova Gulifor Muzaffarovna

© Iskandarova Gulifor Muzzafarovna
Scientific and Practical Research *(Anthology)*
by: Iskandarova Gulifor Muzzafarovna
Edition: May '2025
Publisher:
Taemeer Publications LLC (Michigan, USA / Hyderabad, India)

ISBN 978-93-6908-575-0

© **Iskandarova Gulifor Muzzafarovna**

Book	:	**The Phraseological Units That Shape Our Perception of Life**
Author	:	Iskandarova Gulifor Muzzafarovna
Publisher	:	Taemeer Publications
Year	:	'2025
Pages	:	70
Title Design	:	*Taemeer Web Design*

Table of Contents

Introduction: The Eloquence of the Body …5

Part I: Foundations of Somatic Phraseology …12

Chapter 1: Defining and Classifying Somatic Phraseological Units …12

Chapter 2: Historical Roots and Cultural Evolution …27

Part II: Cognitive and Linguistic Dimensions …31

Chapter 3: Cognitive Processing of Somatic Idioms …31

Chapter 4: Stability, Stereotypes, and Semantic Change …41

Part III: Somatic Idioms in Communication …44

Chapter 5: Idioms in Literature and Media: Usage in Different Contexts ...44

Chapter 6: Digital Age Adaptations: How Idioms are Evolving Online ...48

Part IV: Meaning and Significance ...52

Chapter 7: Idioms and the Meaning of Life: Philosophical connections ...52

Chapter 8: The Future of Somatic Phraseology: Trends and Predictions ...57

Conclusion ...61

References ...65

Introduction: The Eloquence of the Body

Language serves as more than a mere tool for conveying information; it is a dynamic and influential force that actively shapes our understanding of the world around us. At the heart of this transformative power lie phraseological units – those colorful idioms, time-honored proverbs, familiar collocations, and conventional set phrases that enrich our communication and reveal the hidden architecture of thought. These expressions, characterized by their fixed forms and often figurative meanings, transcend the limitations of literal interpretation, offering a glimpse into the shared experiences, cultural values, and cognitive frameworks that define a society. To truly understand how we perceive and interact with the world, we must delve into the fascinating realm of phraseological units and their profound influence on our minds.

Language, far from being a neutral tool for communication, acts as a powerful lens through which we perceive and interpret the world around us. Within the vast landscape of language, phraseological units (PUs) – those colorful, often fixed expressions that pepper our everyday speech – hold a particularly influential position. These units, encompassing idioms, proverbs, collocations, and clichés, are not merely decorative linguistic elements; they actively shape our understanding of reality by encoding cultural values, framing experiences, and subtly influencing our cognitive processes. This essay will explore the profound impact of phraseological units on our perception of life, demonstrating how these seemingly simple expressions contribute to the construction of our individual and collective realities.

Cultural Encoding: Phraseology as a Repository of Shared Values and Beliefs

The intimate relationship between language and culture is a well-established principle in linguistic anthropology. Language serves not only as a means of communication but also as a repository of cultural knowledge, transmitting values, beliefs, and worldviews from one generation to the next. Phraseological units, due to their often-fixed nature and historical roots, are particularly potent carriers of cultural information. They encapsulate a culture's shared experiences, historical events, and deeply held convictions, offering a glimpse into the collective consciousness of a society.

Consider, for instance, the English idiom "to carry coals to Newcastle." This expression, signifying a pointless or redundant activity, derives its meaning from Newcastle's historical prominence as a major coal-mining center. To transport coal to a place already overflowing with it is, quite literally, a futile endeavor. The idiom, therefore, encodes a cultural understanding of efficiency, resourcefulness, and the avoidance of unnecessary effort. Similarly, the proverb "a penny saved is a penny earned" reflects a cultural emphasis on thrift, financial prudence, and the value of hard work. This proverb, common in many Western cultures, promotes a mindset of delayed gratification and careful management of resources.

In contrast, other cultures may prioritize different values, which are reflected in their unique phraseological units. The Spanish saying "El que no llora no mama" ("He who doesn't cry, doesn't get milk") highlights a cultural emphasis on assertiveness, self-advocacy, and the importance of making one's needs known. This contrasts with cultures that may value humility or restraint in expressing one's desires. The Japanese proverb "Deru kugi wa utareru" ("The nail that sticks out gets hammered down") reflects a cultural emphasis on conformity, social harmony, and avoiding standing out from the crowd. These examples illustrate how phraseological units act as cultural markers, providing insights into the values and beliefs that shape a society's worldview.

However, the cultural specificity of phraseological units can also pose challenges in cross-cultural communication. A phrase that is perfectly clear and meaningful within one culture may be completely incomprehensible or even offensive in another. For example, the American idiom "break a leg" (meaning "good luck") could be easily misinterpreted by someone unfamiliar with its figurative meaning. Therefore, a sensitivity to cultural differences in phraseology is crucial for effective intercultural communication and avoiding misunderstandings.

Somatic phraseological units, commonly known as idioms, are linguistic constructs that employ human body-related imagery to convey abstract meanings. They play a fundamental role in English language communication, contributing significantly to the richness and depth of expression. This research paper embarks on a comprehensive exploration of somatic phraseological units in the English language, examining their origins, classifications, cognitive aspects, cultural significance, and contemporary usage. By delving into these multifaceted aspects, we aim to gain a comprehensive understanding of the crucial role somatic idioms play in the English language and the lives of its speakers.

Somatic phraseological units are ubiquitous in the English language, enriching discourse with vivid imagery and cultural connotations. These idiomatic expressions draw inspiration from the human body, offering a unique lens through which speakers convey complex ideas, emotions, and experiences. The study of somatic phraseology in English encompasses various dimensions, from historical origins to contemporary usage, making it a fascinating and rewarding field of linguistic exploration.

Part I: Foundations of Somatic Phraseology

Chapter 1: Defining and Classifying Somatic Phraseological Units

Kunin's Definition and Stability: Exploring the core concepts: As defined by A. V. Kunin, "a phraseological unit is a stable combination of words with fully or partially reinterpreted meaning." This definition underscores the two essential characteristics of phraseological units: stability and idiomaticity. Stability, in this context, refers to the fixed nature of these expressions, indicating that they are typically used in a consistent form and cannot be easily altered without losing their intended meaning.

This stability is based on various types of invariance inherent within the unit, reflecting the invariability of certain elements even amidst normative changes. A. V. Kunin further highlights various types of invariance or microstability that contribute to this overall stability. The stability of a phraseological unit is interpreted as a measure of the degree of semantic cohesion and inseparability of its components. It serves as a form of expression for the idiomatic character specific to that phraseology. In simpler terms, stability acts as a measure of idiomatic character.

Beyond encoding cultural values, phraseological units also play a significant role in framing our experiences and shaping our interpretation of events. Framing, a concept widely used in communication studies and sociology, refers to the process of selecting and highlighting certain aspects of reality while downplaying others, thereby influencing how people understand and respond to events. Phraseological units act as powerful framing devices by providing pre-packaged interpretations of experiences, guiding our attention towards specific aspects of a situation and suggesting particular emotional responses.

Consider the experience of losing a job. This event can be framed in various ways, depending on the phraseological units used to describe it. One might say that the job loss was "a blessing in disguise," framing it as an opportunity for growth, new beginnings, and unforeseen possibilities. This framing emphasizes the potential positive outcomes of the situation, encouraging a sense of optimism and resilience. Alternatively, one might describe the job loss as "having the rug pulled out from under me," framing it as a sudden, unexpected, and potentially devastating betrayal. This framing highlights the feelings of vulnerability, insecurity, and injustice associated with the event.

Similarly, a political debate can be framed in different ways using different phraseological units. Describing a participant as "playing devil's advocate" frames their arguments as a constructive exercise in critical thinking, even if their views are controversial. This framing suggests that the participant is engaging in a valuable intellectual pursuit, challenging assumptions and promoting a deeper understanding of the issues. On the other hand, describing a participant as "beating a dead horse" frames their arguments as a pointless and unproductive endeavor, suggesting that the issue has already been thoroughly discussed and that further debate is futile. This framing discourages further engagement with the topic and dismisses the participant's contributions.

    The framing effects of phraseological units can have a significant impact on our attitudes, beliefs, and behaviors. By shaping our interpretation of events, these expressions can influence our emotional responses, our judgments about others, and our decisions about how to act.

Therefore, it is important to be aware of the framing effects of phraseological units and to critically evaluate the perspectives they promote.

Cognitive Influence: Phraseology and the Way We Think

Cognitive linguistics, a branch of linguistics that emphasizes the role of the mind in shaping language, provides further insights into the profound influence of phraseological units on our cognitive processes. A key concept in cognitive linguistics is the idea of conceptual metaphors, which are underlying cognitive structures that shape our understanding of abstract concepts in terms of more concrete experiences. Many phraseological units are based on these conceptual metaphors, reinforcing certain ways of thinking about the world.

For example, the conceptual metaphor "time is money" is reflected in numerous phraseological units, such as "spending time," "wasting time," "saving time," and "investing time." These expressions lead us to treat time as a valuable resource that can be acquired, managed, and lost, just like money. This metaphor influences our perception of time, encouraging us to be productive, efficient, and to avoid wasting time on frivolous activities.

Another common conceptual metaphor is "arguments are war," which is reflected in phraseological units such as "attacking a point," "defending a position," "shooting down an argument," and "winning an argument." These expressions frame arguments as adversarial battles, where the goal is to defeat one's opponent. This metaphor can influence our approach to disagreements, encouraging us to be aggressive, competitive, and to prioritize winning over understanding.

The repeated use of phraseological units based on certain conceptual metaphors can reinforce certain thought patterns and limit our ability to think about concepts in alternative ways. If we constantly use expressions that frame arguments as wars, we may be less likely to approach disagreements with empathy, collaboration, or a willingness to compromise. Therefore, it is important to be aware of the conceptual metaphors underlying phraseological units and to challenge those that may be limiting our perspectives.

Evolution of Phraseological Theory: A historical overview: The study of phraseological units has garnered attention from numerous scholars and researchers throughout history. The founder of the theory of phraseology is a Swiss linguist, Charles Bally, who is credited with first defining phraseology as an independent section within the broader field of lexicology. Over time, a variety of classifications of phraseological units have been introduced, each offering a unique perspective on their structure and function. V. V. Vinogradov, for instance, divides phraseological units into three distinct types based on the extent to which the nominal values of the components are blurred and the degree to which figurative meaning is present within them.

These categories include phraseological fusions, phraseological units, and phraseological combinations. A.V. Kunin, on the other hand, distinguishes between phraseological units, phraseomatic units, and borderline (mixed) cases, providing a more nuanced classification system. In accordance with Amosova, all phraseological units into phrases and idioms. The absence of at least one of the mentioned features excludes the aforementioned unit from the phraseological structure of the language. Word is the primary, but not only means of nomination in the language system. In speech it is peculiar to appear in combinations with other words, and the principle of their structure in the word combinations is regulated by syntactic norms and rules. Such combinations are created according to the models existing in the language. For example, in English, model A + N, reflecting the fundamental possibility of combining an adjective and a noun, can be filled with an infinite number of components that meet the requirements of the model, and the result of such operation is quite predictable: the resulted combination will indicate something that has a certain feature.

In identical situations, similar phrases are often used: May I come in? Knock at the door, etc. This combination of words is usually used in a fixed form and is reproduced in speech by a ready-made unit. Such combinations are stable, but refer to the general, not the phraseological, fund of the vocabulary. The fact is that there are no semantic changes in the components of such combinations; they preserve their meaning, sometimes changing only the function, as in the stable expression Good morning function is nominative - description of time of day - is replaced by contact - greeting. If stability of an expression is supplemented by semantic changes of a component or components, we deal with a phraseological unit. Despite the fact that phraseological units are combinations of words, they are considered by linguists from the position of lexicology rather than syntax as free combinations. Several reasons are given for this phenomenon.

Primarily, the reason for this is in a free-form word combination created by the model, which can be replaced by any of the components within this model. Thus, adjective red can be used in combination with a huge number of nouns (red frock, red banner, red strip, red hair, etc.), while retaining its color meaning. Similarly, any noun identifying an object potentially capable of having an attribute will, on the same model, be combined with an infinite number of adjectives, this attribute transmitting (red frock, dirty frock, new frock, expensive frock, etc.). In the same phraseological combination, the connection between the components is rigid and the replacement of any of them is impossible without destroying the meaning of the whole unit. For example, the combination black sheep (= the worst member), although it is constructed according to the regular model A + N, cannot be reproduced with the same value even with minimal semantic substitutions (black ram or grey sheep). Formally corresponding to the language model, the phraseological units are not modeled, i.e., they represent a single use of the language model to transmit in a constant context any semantic structure.

Somatic Idiom Classification: A detailed look at types: Somatic phraseological units can be categorized into various types based on their structural and semantic properties. This classification includes:

- Simple somatic idioms are those expressions that contain a single body-related element, typically a body part or a bodily action. Examples: "Head over heels" - This idiom refers to being deeply in love or infatuated. The body part, "head," is used in conjunction with the action of being "over heels" to convey the intensity of the emotion. "Cold feet" - This expression means apprehension or reluctance. The body part, "feet," symbolizes one's physical hesitation or nervousness. Significance: Simple somatic idioms provide concise and vivid imagery, making them easily recognizable and memorable. They often encapsulate common human experiences and emotions.

- Compound somatic idioms are more complex expressions that combine multiple body related elements within the same phrase. Examples: "Heart of gold" - In this idiom, two body-related elements, "heart" and "gold," are combined to symbolize a person's kind and generous nature. "Butterflies in the stomach" - This expression uses "butterflies" and "stomach" to convey the sensation of nervousness or excitement. Significance: Compound somatic idioms often create more nuanced or layered meanings by juxtaposing different body-related elements. They can be particularly effective in conveying abstract concepts.

o Metaphorical somatic idioms use body-related imagery metaphorically to convey abstract concepts or emotions. Examples: "Grasping at straws" - This idiom employs the metaphor of "grasping" to represent someone making desperate or futile attempts to find a solution. "Breaking the ice" - Here, "breaking" is used metaphorically to describe the act of initiating a conversation to relieve tension or awkwardness. Significance: Metaphorical somatic idioms offer a rich and figurative way to express abstract ideas. They enable speakers to vividly convey complex concepts by drawing on universally understood physical actions or sensations.

o Non-metaphorical somatic idioms maintain a direct and literal connection between the body-related imagery and the intended meaning. Examples: "Raising one's eyebrows" - In this idiom, the action of "raising one's eyebrows" directly corresponds to expressing surprise, skepticism, or disapproval. "Rolling one's eyes" - Here, the literal action of "rolling one's eyes" is synonymous with expressing annoyance or disbelief. Significance: Non-metaphorical somatic idioms rely on the physical actions or reactions associated with the body parts involved. They are often used to describe nonverbal communication or emotional responses in a straightforward manner. Understanding these classifications allows linguists, language learners, and researchers to systematically analyze somatic phraseological units in English. It provides a framework for dissecting the structural and semantic properties of idiomatic expressions, shedding light on how these linguistic constructs contribute to the richness and nuance of the English language.

Chapter 2: Historical Roots and Cultural Evolution

Body as Metaphor Source: The origins of somatic idioms: The historical roots of somatic phraseological units can be traced back to the earliest stages of human language development. As humans evolved and developed increasingly complex communication systems, they naturally drew upon their immediate physical experiences, particularly those related to their bodies, to describe abstract concepts, emotions, and experiences.

Early humans relied on their bodily sensations and actions as a primary source of metaphorical language. This approach was not only practical but also highly intuitive. When they experienced strong emotions or encountered novel situations, they turned to the physical sensations they could perceive and the actions they could perform to create metaphors that vividly conveyed their inner experiences to others.

Case Study: "Heavy Heart": A deeper analysis: One compelling example of this historical process is the idiom "to have a heavy heart." In this expression, the human heart, a vital organ central to life and emotions, is used metaphorically to convey the sensation of sadness or emotional burden.

The idiom suggests that the weight of sorrow is similar to the actual physical sensation of heaviness in the chest area. This idiom reflects a deep connection between the physical world and the emotional realm. Early speakers of the English language recognized that the physical sensations associated with certain emotions, such as sadness or grief, were akin to the tangible experience of carrying a heavy object on one's chest. As a result, they harnessed this metaphorical link to create a powerful and universally understandable expression.

Cultural Influence on Idioms: The role of society and history: Understanding the historical roots of somatic phraseological units provides valuable insights into their enduring significance. These expressions are not arbitrary; they are rooted in the very fabric of human experience and perception. They capture the essence of what it means to be human and to communicate complex emotions and abstract ideas. Even as language evolves and societies change, somatic phraseological units remain relevant and resonant because they tap into a fundamental aspect of the human condition.

They remind us that our bodies have always served as a source of inspiration and metaphor, allowing us to bridge the gap between the tangible and the intangible, the physical and the emotional. In essence, somatic phraseological units in English are a testament to the creative and imaginative nature of human language, forever linking the physical world to the realm of language and emotion. Their historical roots enrich our understanding of the depth and universality of these linguistic constructs, underscoring their enduring significance in our daily communication and cultural heritage.

Part II: Cognitive and Linguistic Dimensions

Chapter 3: Cognitive Processing of Somatic Idioms

Cognitive Linguistics and Interpretation: How we understand idioms:

The cognitive processing of somatic idioms constitutes a rich and compelling area of study, dedicated to unraveling the intricate mental mechanisms that underpin our ability to comprehend and employ these pervasive figurative expressions. Cognitive linguistics, a prominent branch of linguistics that emphasizes the central role of the human mind in shaping and structuring language, provides a robust and insightful framework for investigating this multifaceted cognitive terrain.

Cognitive linguists embark on a detailed exploration of the complex processes involved in the interpretation of idiomatic language. This investigation scrutinizes how our minds navigate the inherent gap between the literal, compositional meanings of individual words and the more abstract, holistic concepts that they collectively represent within the context of an idiom. This exploration extends beyond mere semantic analysis, delving into how our embodied experiences, sensorimotor knowledge, and deeply ingrained conceptual metaphors fundamentally underpin our understanding and fluent processing of these expressions.

Furthermore, cognitive linguistic approaches examine how the brain actively constructs meaning during idiom comprehension, often drawing upon contextual cues, prior knowledge, and pragmatic inferences to resolve potential ambiguities and arrive at the intended interpretation. Researchers investigate the degree to which idioms are processed as holistic units versus compositional structures, exploring the neural correlates associated with each processing strategy. By integrating insights from psychology, neuroscience, and computer science, cognitive linguistics offers a comprehensive and dynamic perspective on how we seamlessly bridge the gap between literal language and figurative meaning in the realm of somatic idioms, shedding light on the intricate interplay between language, thought, embodiment, and the human capacity for abstract reasoning.

Key Principles of Cognitive Linguistics in Idiom Interpretation:

o **Embodied Cognition:** This principle suggests that our understanding of language is grounded in our physical experiences and bodily interactions with the world. Somatic idioms, which draw directly on body-related imagery, are prime examples of embodied cognition in action. Our understanding of idioms like "cold feet" or "butterflies in the stomach" is rooted in our actual physical sensations and experiences. "Cold feet," for example, doesn't just mean that someone's feet are literally cold; it taps into the feeling of nervousness and anxiety that can manifest as physical sensations, including a chill or a feeling of wanting to retreat. "Butterflies in the stomach" similarly connects the abstract feeling of nervousness or excitement to a physical sensation that many people have experienced.

o **Conceptual Metaphor:** Conceptual

metaphor theory, pioneered by George Lakoff and Mark Johnson, posits that abstract concepts are understood in terms of more concrete ones through the use of metaphors. Many idioms are based on underlying conceptual metaphors, such as "ARGUMENT IS WAR" (e.g., "He attacked my position") or "TIME IS MONEY" (e.g., "I'm running out of time"). These metaphors provide a cognitive framework for understanding the abstract meanings of idioms. For instance, the ARGUMENT IS WAR metaphor allows us to understand debates and disagreements as battles, with participants taking "positions," "attacking" opposing viewpoints, and "defending" their own. This metaphor is deeply ingrained in how we think and talk about arguments.

- **Mental Imagery:** Mental imagery plays a crucial role in idiom comprehension. When we encounter an idiom, our minds often create a mental image associated with the literal meaning of the words. This image then serves as a bridge to the abstract meaning of the idiom. For example, when we hear the idiom "break the ice," we might first visualize someone literally breaking a sheet of ice. This image then helps us understand the idiom's meaning of initiating a conversation to relieve tension or awkwardness. The ability to create and manipulate mental images is a key component of our cognitive ability to understand figurative language.

Contextual Factors in Idiom Interpretation:

- **Situational Context:** The context in which an idiom is used provides crucial clues to its intended meaning. The surrounding words, the speaker's tone, and the overall situation all contribute to our understanding. For example, the idiom "hit the roof" can have different meanings depending on the context. If someone says, "I was so angry, I hit the roof!", it means they became extremely angry. However, if someone says, "The company's profits hit the roof this quarter!", it means the profits increased dramatically.

- **Cultural Context:** Idioms are often culturally specific, and their meanings can vary across different cultures. Understanding the cultural context is essential for accurate interpretation. For example, the idiom "to kick the bucket" is a common euphemism for death in English-speaking cultures, but it might not be understood in the same way in other cultures.

- **Prior Knowledge:** Our prior knowledge and experiences also influence how we interpret idioms. The more familiar we are with a particular idiom, the easier it is to understand its meaning. We also draw on our general knowledge of the world and our understanding of social conventions to make inferences about the intended meaning of idioms.

Neurological Aspects of Idiom Processing:

o   Neuroimaging studies have revealed that different areas of the brain are involved in processing idioms compared to literal language. These studies have shown that the right hemisphere of the brain plays a significant role in understanding figurative language, including idioms.

o   Research also suggests that the brain activates both literal and figurative meanings of idioms initially, and then selects the appropriate meaning based on context. This process involves complex interactions between different brain regions.

Conceptual Metaphor Theory: Underlying cognitive structures: Phraseological units are not simply decorative elements of language; they are deeply intertwined with our cognitive processes, shaping how we think, remember, and understand the world. Conceptual Metaphor Theory (Lakoff & Johnson, 1980) posits that our understanding of abstract concepts is grounded in concrete experiences through the use of metaphors. Many idioms are based on these underlying conceptual metaphors. For example:

o   ARGUMENT IS WAR: "He attacked my position," "She shot down my argument," "I won the debate."

o   TIME IS MONEY: "I'm running out of time," "Don't waste my time," "Time is precious."

o   IDEAS ARE FOOD: "That's food for thought," "I can't digest that idea," "He has a taste for abstract concepts." These metaphors shape how we reason about and value different aspects of life.

Mental Lexicon and Storage: How idioms are stored in the brain: The fixed nature of phraseological units makes them easier to remember and retrieve from memory. This is because they are stored as single units in our mental lexicon, rather than being constructed from individual words each time we encounter them. This allows us to process information more efficiently and communicate more effectively. The more frequently we encounter a phraseological unit, the stronger its representation in our memory becomes.

Chapter 4: Stability, Stereotypes, and Semantic Change

Stability and Invariance: The characteristics of idioms: As defined by A. V. Kunin, "a phraseological unit is a stable combination of words with fully or partially reinterpreted meaning". It points to stability as one of the FE criteria. This stability is based on various types of invariance inherent in it, i.e., invariability of certain elements at all-normative changes. A. V. Kunin highlights the following types of invariance or microstability: The stability of a phraseological unit is interpreted as a measure, the degree of semantic cohesion and inseparability of components. It is a form of expression of idiomatic character with specific phraseology. In other words, stability is a measure of idiomatic character.

Cultural Stereotypes in Idioms: The impact of societal biases: Since phraseology is connected with a stereotype, then it is phraseology that is the means of expressing this stereotype, which is connected with a certain representation or image expressed in this phraseology. In cognitive linguistics and ethnolinguistics the term stereotype refers to the content side of language and culture, i.e. it is understood as a mental stereotype that is associated with the linguistic picture of the world. In E.V. Bartminsky's case the language picture of the world and the language stereotype are treated as a part and whole, and the language stereotype is understood as "a judgment or several judgments related to a certain object of the extra-linguistic world, subjectively deterministic representation of the subject, in which descriptive and evaluation characteristics coexist and which is the result of interpretation of reality within the framework of socially developed cognitive models".

Semantic Evolution: How idioms change over

time: Phraseological units are not simply decorative elements of language; they are deeply intertwined with our cognitive processes, shaping how we think, remember, and understand the world.

Part III: Somatic Idioms in Communication

Chapter 5: Idioms in Literature and Media: Usage in Different Contexts

Somatic phraseological units are far from being relics of a bygone era or confined to dusty dictionaries; they remain an integral and vibrant part of modern English language communication. Their enduring presence and adaptability are a testament to their power and versatility. These expressive idioms seamlessly weave their way into the fabric of our daily lives, finding their place in a diverse array of contexts, from the most casual of everyday conversations to the carefully crafted narratives of literature, the persuasive pitches of advertising, and the dynamic landscape of digital communication.

The ubiquity of somatic idioms underscores their importance in conveying meaning, adding nuance, and engaging audiences. They are not merely decorative elements of language; they are essential tools for expressing complex ideas, emotions, and experiences in a concise and memorable way.

In everyday conversations, somatic idioms add color and personality to our interactions. They allow us to express ourselves in a more vivid and relatable manner, connecting with others on a deeper level. For example, saying "I'm feeling under the weather" is a more expressive way of saying "I'm not feeling well," conveying a sense of vulnerability and inviting empathy.

In literature, authors strategically employ somatic idioms to create vivid imagery, develop characters, and enhance the overall impact of their stories. Idioms can be used to reveal a character's personality, to set the tone of a scene, or to explore deeper themes. The strategic use of idioms can elevate a literary work from the ordinary to the extraordinary.

In advertising, somatic idioms are used to capture attention, create memorable slogans, and persuade consumers to take action. Advertisers understand the power of idioms to resonate with audiences on an emotional level, tapping into shared cultural understandings and creating a sense of connection.

In the ever-evolving world of digital communication, somatic idioms are adapting to new forms of expression, including emojis, GIFs, and memes. These visual elements add a new layer of meaning to idioms, allowing for even more nuanced and expressive communication.

This chapter will delve into the specific ways in which somatic idioms are used in each of these contexts, exploring their unique functions and effects. We will examine how idioms are employed in literature to create compelling narratives, how they are used in advertising to persuade consumers, and how they are evolving in the digital age to meet the demands of online communication. By exploring these diverse contexts, we will gain a deeper appreciation for the enduring power and versatility of somatic phraseological units in the English language.

Chapter 6: Digital Age Adaptations: How Idioms are Evolving Online

The digital age, with its unprecedented speed of communication and its constantly shifting technological landscape, has profoundly impacted the way we use language. This impact is particularly evident in the adaptation of somatic idioms to social media platforms, where these expressive phrases continue to play a crucial role in shaping the way we articulate emotions, share ideas, and connect with one another in a rapidly evolving linguistic landscape.

Social media platforms, such as Twitter, Facebook, Instagram, TikTok, and countless others, have become virtual town squares where individuals from all walks of life gather to exchange information, express opinions, and build relationships. Within these digital spaces, language is constantly evolving, adapting to the unique constraints and opportunities presented by the online environment.

Somatic idioms, with their inherent expressiveness and cultural resonance, have proven to be remarkably adaptable to this new environment. However, their adaptation is not merely a simple transplantation from offline to online contexts. Instead, these idioms are undergoing a fascinating transformation, shaped by the unique characteristics of social media, including its emphasis on brevity, visual communication, and rapid dissemination of information.

On social media platforms, idioms are often shortened, abbreviated, or combined with emojis and GIFs to convey meaning in a more concise and visually appealing manner. For example, the idiom "facepalm" has spawned a plethora of emoji and GIF variations, allowing users to express frustration or disbelief with a single click.

Moreover, social media has also given rise

to entirely new somatic idioms that reflect the unique experiences and challenges of online life. Terms like "going viral," "trolling," "ghosting," and "doomscrolling" have quickly become part of the digital lexicon, capturing the essence of online phenomena in a vivid and memorable way.

This chapter will delve into the specific ways in which somatic idioms are adapting to the digital age, exploring their evolution on social media platforms and examining the emergence of new idioms that reflect the online world. We will analyze the impact of visual communication, the role of brevity, and the influence of social media culture on the transformation of these expressive phrases. By understanding these adaptations, we can gain a deeper appreciation for the dynamic and ever-changing nature of language in the digital age. We will also consider the implications of these changes for communication, culture, and identity in an increasingly interconnected world.

Part IV: Meaning and Significance
Chapter 7: Idioms and the Meaning of Life: Philosophical connections

Many major historical figures in philosophy have provided an answer to the question of what, if anything, makes life meaningful, although they typically have not put it in these terms (with such talk having arisen only in the past 250 years or so, on which see Landau 1997). Consider, for instance, Aristotle on the human function, Aquinas on the beatific vision, and Kant on the highest good. Relatedly, think about Koheleth, the presumed author of the Biblical book Ecclesiastes, describing life as "futility" and akin to "the pursuit of wind," Nietzsche on nihilism, as well as Schopenhauer when he remarks that whenever we reach a goal we have longed for we discover "how vain and empty it is." While these concepts have some bearing on happiness and virtue (and their opposites), they are straightforwardly construed (roughly) as accounts of which highly ranked purposes a person ought to realize that would make her life significant (if any would).

Despite the venerable pedigree, it is only since the 1980s or so that a distinct field of the meaning of life has been established in Anglo-American-Australasian philosophy, on which this survey focuses, and it is only in the past 20 years that debate with real depth and intricacy has appeared. Two decades ago analytic reflection on life's meaning was described as a "backwater" compared to that on well-being or good character, and it was possible to cite nearly all the literature in a given critical discussion of the field (Metz 2002). Neither is true any longer. Anglo-American-Australasian philosophy of life's meaning has become vibrant, such that there is now way too much literature to be able to cite comprehensively in this survey. To obtain focus, it tends to discuss books, influential essays, and more recent works, and it leaves aside contributions from other philosophical traditions (such as the Continental or African) and from non-philosophical fields (e.g., psychology or literature). This survey's central aim is to acquaint the reader with current analytic approaches to life's meaning, sketching major debates and pointing out neglected topics that merit further consideration.

When the topic of the meaning of life comes up, people tend to pose one of three questions: "What are you talking about?", "What is the meaning of life?", and "Is life in fact meaningful?". The literature on life's meaning composed by those working in the analytic tradition (on which this entry focuses) can be usefully organized according to which question it seeks to answer. This survey starts off with recent work that addresses the first, abstract (or "meta") question regarding the sense of talk of "life's meaning," i.e., that aims to clarify what we have in mind when inquiring into the meaning of life. Afterward, it considers texts that provide answers to the more substantive question about the nature of meaningfulness. There is in the making a subfield of applied meaning that parallels applied ethics, in which meaningfulness is considered in the context of particular cases or specific themes. Examples include downshifting (Levy 2005), implementing genetic enhancements (Agar 2013), making achievements (Bradford 2015), getting an education (Schinkel et al. 2015), interacting with research participants (Olson 2016), automating labor (Danaher 2017), and creating children (Ferracioli 2018). In contrast, this survey focuses nearly exclusively on contemporary normative-theoretical approaches to life's meanining, that is, attempts to capture in a single, general principle all the variegated conditions that could confer meaning on life. Finally, this survey examines fresh arguments for the nihilist view that the conditions necessary for a meaningful life do not obtain for any of us, i.e., that all our lives are meaningless.

Chapter 8: The Future of Somatic Phraseology: Trends and Predictions

The study of somatic phraseological units in English is far more than a simple exercise in linguistic analysis; it represents a multifaceted exploration that encompasses historical, structural, cognitive, cultural, and contemporary dimensions. These idiomatic expressions, drawing their power and resonance from the human body, are not merely linguistic constructs to be dissected and categorized. Instead, they serve as invaluable windows into the very essence of human experiences, offering profound insights into our shared cultural values, and revealing the intricate ways in which we perceive and interact with the world around us.

By delving deeply into the fascinating realm of somatic phraseology, linguists, researchers, and language enthusiasts alike embark on a journey of discovery, gaining a far deeper appreciation for the inherent artistry and complexity that underlie the seemingly simple words we use to communicate in the English language. This exploration allows us to move beyond a superficial understanding of language and to recognize the rich tapestry of meaning woven into these expressions.

Consider, for example, the historical dimension. Tracing the origins of somatic idioms reveals how our ancestors used their understanding of the body to describe abstract concepts, emotions, and social relationships. These idioms often reflect the beliefs, values, and practices of past generations, providing a tangible link to our cultural heritage.

The structural dimension highlights the unique grammatical and semantic properties of somatic idioms. These expressions often defy the rules of literal language, employing figurative language, metaphor, and metonymy to create meaning. Understanding the structural characteristics of idioms allows us to appreciate their creative and expressive power.

The cognitive dimension explores how our minds process and interpret somatic idioms. Cognitive linguistics sheds light on the mental mechanisms involved in understanding figurative language, revealing how we draw on our embodied experiences and conceptual metaphors to make sense of idiomatic expressions.

The cultural dimension emphasizes the role of culture in shaping the meaning and use of somatic idioms. Idioms are often deeply embedded in cultural contexts, reflecting the values, beliefs, and social norms of a particular community. Understanding the cultural context is essential for accurate interpretation and effective communication.

Finally, the contemporary dimension examines how somatic idioms are used in modern

English, including their adaptation to new technologies and social media platforms. This exploration reveals the dynamic and evolving nature of language, as idioms adapt to changing cultural landscapes.

In essence, the study of somatic phraseology is a journey that takes us from the historical roots of language to the cutting edge of contemporary communication. It is a journey that deepens our understanding of the human condition and celebrates the power of language to shape our thoughts, emotions, and experiences. As we look to the future, it is essential to continue this exploration, recognizing that somatic phraseology is not just a collection of words, but a living, breathing reflection of who we are as human beings.

Conclusion

In conclusion, phraseological units (PUs) stand as far more than mere colorful embellishments to our language; they are, in essence, foundational building blocks of our cognitive and cultural frameworks, wielding a remarkably significant and often underestimated influence over the very fabric of how we perceive, interpret, and ultimately interact with the world around us. Their impact resonates far beyond the superficial realm of simple communication, reaching deep into the core of our understanding. They actively shape our comprehension of deeply ingrained cultural values, meticulously frame our interpretations of the myriad events that unfold in our lives, and subtly yet powerfully guide our thought processes through the pervasive presence of conceptual metaphors that have become so deeply embedded within our linguistic landscape that we often fail to recognize their influence.

The importance of recognizing and appreciating the profound power of these seemingly innocuous expressions cannot be overstated. It is absolutely paramount for fostering not only effective and clear communication but also for promoting genuine and meaningful cross-cultural understanding, bridging divides that might otherwise seem insurmountable. Furthermore, this awareness is crucial for cultivating and honing critical thinking skills, enabling us to analyze information with a discerning eye and to challenge assumptions that might otherwise go unexamined. As we embark on a journey to become more attuned to the intricate and often subtle ways in which phraseological units shape our thoughts, perceptions, and biases, we simultaneously empower ourselves to engage with the world in a far more nuanced, empathetic, and comprehensively informed manner.

By consciously and deliberately choosing our language, carefully considering the implications of the words and phrases we employ, and critically evaluating the underlying assumptions that are often subtly embedded within these expressions, we can actively participate in shaping our own individual realities. This conscious effort allows us to move beyond passively accepting pre-packaged interpretations and to actively construct our own understanding of the world. Moreover, by embracing this linguistic awareness, we contribute to fostering a world where communication transcends the mere exchange of information and evolves into a powerful catalyst for deeper understanding, stronger connection, and the creation of shared meaning that enriches the human experience.

In this ongoing and ever-evolving journey of linguistic awareness, we come to a profound realization: the phrases we use are not simply passive reflections of the world as it exists around us; rather, they are active and dynamic agents in its continuous creation, constantly shaping and reshaping our understanding of reality and influencing the course of human interaction. They are the invisible threads that weave together our individual and collective narratives, and by understanding their power, we gain the ability to become more conscious and deliberate authors of our own stories and of the world we wish to create.

REFERENCES

1. Crystal, D. (1997). *English as a global language.* Cambridge University Press.

2. Gibbs, R. W., Jr. (1994). *The poetics of mind: Figurative thought, language, and understanding.* Cambridge University Press.

3. Moon, R. (1998). *Fixed expressions and idioms in English: A corpus-based approach.* Oxford University Press.

4. Nunberg, G. (1979). *The non-transformational syntax of gerunds.* Linguistic Inquiry Monographs, MIT Press.

5. Partington, A. (1998). *Patterns and meanings: Using corpora for English language research and teaching.* John Benjamins Publishing.

6. Steen, G. J. (2007). Finding metaphor in discourse: Pragmatics and beyond. In D. Geeraerts & H. Cuyckens (Eds.), *The Oxford handbook of cognitive linguistics.* Oxford

University Press.

7. Zoltán, K. (2006). *Language, mind, and culture: A practical introduction.* Oxford University Press.

8. Alimov, V. V. (2005). *Theoretical translation. Translation in the field of professional communication: textbook.* URSS.

9. Chuzhakin, A. P., & Palazhchenko, P. R. (1999). *The world of translation, or the eternal search for mutual understanding.* Valent.

10. Schweitzer, A. D. (2012). *Through the eyes of a translator: from memories.* R. Valent.

11. Sadykova, A. G., Kajumova, D. F., Demirag, D. N., Aleeva, G. K., Tulusina, E. A., Zinnatova, D. M., & Yagmurova, M. S. (2024). The usage of phraseological units of the English language with an onomastic component in speeches of political figures (a study of political discourse). *Cadernos de Educação Tecnologia e*

Sociedade, 17(1), 414-423. https://doi.org/10.14571/brajets.v17.n1.414-423

12. Alimov, V. V. (2005). *Theoretical translation. Translation in the field of professional communication: textbook.* URSS.

13. Chuzhakin, A. P., & Palazhchenko, P. R. (1999). *The world of translation, or the eternal search for mutual understanding.* Valent.

14. Schweitzer, A. D. (2012). *Through the eyes of a translator: from memories.* R. Valent.

15. Alimov, V. V. (2005). *Theoretical translation. Translation in the field of professional communication: textbook.* URSS.

16. Chuzhakin, A. P., & Palazhchenko, P. R. (1999). *The world of translation, or the eternal search for mutual understanding.* Valent.

17. Schweitzer, A. D. (2012). *Through the eyes of a translator: from memories.* R. Valent.

18. Kunin, A. V. (1984). *Anglo-russkiy frazeologicheskiy slovar' [English-Russian phraseological dictionary]*. Russkiy yazyk.

19. Ozhegov, S. I. (1987). *Slovar' russkogo yazyka [Dictionary of the Russian language]*. Russkiy yazyk.

20. Teliya, V. N. (1996). *Russkaya frazeologiya [Russian phraseology]*.

21. Ganshina, K. A. (1971). *Frantsuzsko-russkiy slovar' [French-Russian dictionary]*. Sovetskaya entsiklopediya.

22. Bírová, J. (2013). About theoretical definitions of pluralistic and Pluricultural approaches. *XLinguae, European Scientific Language Journal, 6*(2), 91-103.

23. Tairova, F. (2021). The notion of phraseological unit. *Vestnik Kyrgyzskogo gosudarstvennogo universiteta im. I. Arabaeva, 7*(1), Retrieved from https://doi.org/10.33619/2414-2948/62

24. The Meaning of Life. (2021, February 9). *Stanford Encyclopedia of Philosophy*. Retrieved from (Original Publication Date: May 15, 2007)

25. Landau, I. (1997). Why has the question of the meaning of life arisen in the last two and a half centuries? *Philosophy Today, 41*, 263–270.

26. Nietzsche, F. (1954). *Thus spoke Zarathustra* (W. Kaufmann, Ed. & Trans.). Viking Press. (Original work published 1885)

27. Metz, T. (2002). Recent work on the meaning of life. *Ethics, 112*, 781–814.

28. Metz, T. (2013). *Meaning in life: An analytic study*. Oxford University Press.

29. Levy, N. (2005). Downshifting and meaning in life. *Ratio, 18*, 176–189.

30. Agar, N. (2013). *Humanity's end: Why we should reject radical enhancement*. MIT Press.

31. Bradford, G. (2015). *Achievement.* Oxford University Press.

32. Schinkel, A., De Ruyter, D., & Aviram, A. (2015). Education and life's meaning. *Journal of Philosophy of Education, 50*, 398–418.

33. Olson, N. (2016). Medical researchers' ancillary care obligations. *Bioethics, 30*, 317–324.

34. Danaher, J. (2017). Will life be worth living in a world without work? Technological unemployment and the meaning of life. *Science and Engineering Ethics, 23*, 41–64.

35. Ferracioli, L. (2018). Procreative-parenting, Love's Reasons, and the Demands of Morality. *The Philosophical Quarterly, 68*, 77–97.

www.ingramcontent.com/pod-product-compliance
Lightning Source LLC
LaVergne TN
LVHW021303080526
838199LV00090B/6001